Doubra I

MY BOOK OF POEMS

MY BOOK OF POEMS

By

Doubra Fufeyin

Dedication

To

This book is dedicated to the memory of
Ibidunni Ajayi Ituah- Ighodalo
whose death spurred the putting together of this
book.

Doubra Fufeyin: My Book of Poems

IF MY THOUGHTS

If my thoughts are shared in its purest form; if I can convey meaning through imagery, rhyme and verse, then this gift, with which I have been blessed, shall not die with me but will come alive, each time a page of this book is turned.

Doubra Fufeyin.

Preface

I fell in love with words at an early age, and I think that my father was partly and mostly responsible for that. He was surrounded by books from encyclopedias and several genres of literature ranging from history and religion to art. It was a good way to feed my curious mind. My favourite pastime was to sit by his foot and have him dish out different words for me to spell.

Occasionally, I challenged him because I had read my dictionary in and out. By far my greatest disappointment came when he asked me to spell the word "etiquette" and without a care, I rambled on to spell air ticket. That was my first lesson on homonyms. (Words that sound alike but are spelt differently).

As I grew older, I started to write down my thoughts, blended it with imagery, rhyme and verse. The rest is history, for little did I know that my imagination would merge with my experiences to become a source of expression and fulfillment. They say that your passion is your drive and when you are driven, your passion ignites your fire.

v

The fire in my soul, in my mind, in my heart comes alive when I write poetry. In reality, the greatest question is why are we here? And where are we headed? In between this journey of self-realization, uncertainties unravel and in trying to solve the puzzles, I find myself putting down views, so it is now a part of me. For what started as a mere expression of thoughts has now become an undying passion that is here to stay.

Doubra Fufeyin.
18 June 2020

Contents

Doubra Fufeyin: My Book of Poems

VICTIM OF BEAUTY

A face that strikes, a smile that speaks, body of a goddess,
epitome of charm and grace.

Where is thy sting? beneath the exterior that makes men drool.

Let not your looks be your weapon for when it fades
thou shalt be naked.

For deep in the heart lies the real woman, conscious of life
and ready to fight the battles that must come.

She brings to life, she supports because she knows her role
on the stage of life.

This is why she holds her head up high and beats her chest in unison saying: 'I shall not be a victim of beauty.'

THE LOST ONES[1]

For some reason it started.
They fought and it lasted.
Then their lives were wasted.
In the dailies pictures painted.
It does not remove the sorrow,
But we will not wallow
But stand to remember a void so hollow.

LOVE CHILD

Her blue eyes with a hint of hazel gleamed as she looked at the
clear blue sky oblivious to how she had been made.
Her rich velvety caramel skin shone against the rays that
shimmered through the window.
She held out delicate hands wanting to be held, but instead he
stroked her curly brown hair peppered with streaks of gold.
She had the same smile that struck the chord that dark
November's day.
He was sure the nose was his, but the smile was definitely hers,

---

[1] *Written on 4th August 2014*
To commemorate the WW1 centenary

the enchanted smile he fell in love with.
He smiled as he became gripped by emotions that
he knew only
too well.
Just then she kicked her endless legs in the air as
she cooed and
babbled in response to his touch.
And just he knew that he was blessed to have
harnessed the
moment when this journey began.

AUTUMN CHILL

It's brutally windy, yet the sun is out. As I boldly
decide what best to wear I am choosing wisely
least I have a Marilyn Monroe moment with
hands flaying about to hold down my flying skirt
that has decided like Scarlett O' Hara to go with
the wind. It's bright and dull, leaves about and
hair in my face. I relish the end of summer and
the dawn of winter.

Seasons come and go more reasons to start
anew. Mixed feelings too surreal to forget
yet too real to dismiss. I hold my head to
imbibe it all, for change must come
regardless of what I feel. Head above
water, shoulders square, steady like a soldier's
gait. Rising to occasion, for the chill of autumn I
must embrace.

I AM THE CRAY

I am rich in ancestry and history.
Scenery and greenery boundless and limitless.
I am full of heritage and with age evolved with
beauty and dignity through art, music and prose.
To this day, I uphold my totality with a lot more
presence, my essence shall not wither nor be a
forgotten tale of the past.
Indeed, I am blest to flourish, yes I nourish a
generation Already born ready to bloom in the
Cray.

THE WAR OF THE STARS

I do not think I have been guided by the stars
every step of the way. Let's just say that I have
been intrigued by the accuracy of the Zodiac's
definition of character. I like everyone has hoped
for greatness by carving a path to launch my very
existence, with every milestone deepening my
hunger of an insatiable thirst. At first, the grill
becomes a thrill releasing bursts of satisfaction
affirming every action. Till I meet the traffic that
makes one feel you are neither coming nor going.
Through it all, the answer lies within. It has
always been the case during the chase. To pause
and decipher the cause.

In the end, I realize that I might not, like Grace
Kelly or Meghan Markle, add sparkle to my life
through royalty. After all I am of the tribe of

Lion of Judah. I am content knowing that adding a sparkle to those around me might just be all that I need to feel royal and loyal.

One fine day looking through old photos, recapturing memories of yesteryears, one picture struck a chord. On the first day my son was born, while still trying to adapt to his new world, his outfit read 'England's future footballer'. At this point he laughed out loud saying: "Mum you got one point wrong I am going to play for Nigeria." It was a surreal moment that made me feel my work here is done, if I can raise a son who regardless of where he was born knows his roots, or a daughter who excels academically regardless of the colour of her skin, if they can embrace friendship in one and all and accept the supremacy of our creator. Then yes I am fine, just being that sparkle that makes that much of a difference.

ELEMENTS OF TIME

What do you do with your time?
You can do anything with it
Just remember time is watching you.
Whenever it comes, and wherever it goes. It goes by so quickly and you don't even know.
Whenever it comes back to visit, remember when I told you.

Time is watching you . Eva Idunorba[2]

WRITER'S PARADISE.

I live in a writer's paradise and this I know for sure. Whether I look through the window or I step out my front door. There is something to be struck by. A sunrise or the sun at dusk. I remain mesmerized by the breeze in the trees, I freeze and admire its lushness it's all green all the way down to green street green.

One morning I woke up to the blanket of fog that had formed a haze on the houses and the fields across from my gaze. The fields are bare, and the adjoining streets are bare also. Windows and curtains showing that people are rousing from the night before. To start the day, another day that cannot tell how it's going to end.

The view from my roof top is picturesque. A view that would have been van Gogh's delight. I picture him stroking away and humming to with the birds as they break into a song that you cannot help but notice. It is a sight to behold, a scenery with greenery that can make anyone green with envy. It is what it is and it is my writer's paradise.

---

[2] *(daughter of the Poet)*

WOMAN'S WORTH.

What is the value of a woman with beauty
without a heart? With a heart but no one to love.
With love and no one to share it with. With child
but no food to give or with food no health to
enjoy. With health but no one to bless.
Let the woman that is worthy step forward for all
the world to see. There will be a stand still
because they are women and there are women.
Blessed beyond words, favored in eyes of God.
Those hands hardened by hard work will see
softness in her lifetime.
Those doors she thought were shut forever will
be open for business. The business of the day
will be to boldly step out in faith armed with God
given talents and passions. Alas! She will laugh
and dance to music of her youth, basking in the
prestige and honor that is her award. She will
smile and say that the lord is good.

AFRICAN PRINCESS

I am a princess, true the daughter of the soil. My
brown skin, my brown eyes, a reflection of my
being. Childbearing hips that sway with promise,
neck of a gazelle, arms that show strength. A
bosom where comfort is assured and a back that
has borne the weight of motherhood.
I am a guardian, a custodian of values,
entrenched in history which i pass to generations

7

unborn. I am a symbol of hope and a torch in a decaying society, where left, right and Centre. The debate at the epicentre is what lives matter. Mine or that of the light skinned boy that lives down the street. I was made in Africa, made in Nigeria, south south in the Niger delta. Now an export in the so-called western part of the world. As I try to maintain my sanity as to which side of the globe makes me more of who I am. I must remind myself. That I bear the mark of fortitude and in gratitude, remember that I am a silent force that must sing like the lion in Zion.

MY CROSS

Let me carry my cross for it will be lighter than the weight of the world. Let them talk and laugh as I speed past with a blast, to a zone where I shall find comfort, while mere mortals wonder and ponder.

My creator sets my foot to a place where I have never been. As I begin, I begin this journey, I can see that it is going to be as bright as a rainbow after a thunderstorm.

I CRY FOR MY DELTA

Alas! I am back to my roots, for the earth has opened for a son to come. He slumbers and he shall never wake. As I begin my journey, my mind is geared towards that which I must come to terms with, the reality I may not want to accept, the reality that is reality. As we move towards my regions, there is a gradual diminishing stare that hits me in the face and every move is a deviation from modern day structures and infrastructure.

The solace of plantation, swamps and the beauty of nature gives way to water. That is when your mind begins to wonder into space because that is mostly what you will find. It is not a tourists dream, floating aquatic life poisoned by contaminated water bodies, destruction of farmlands, the black oil that spilled into rivers and creeks for weeks on end.

Their greatest gift is their poison extracted to enrich others while they wallow in squalor, with little or nothing to hold unto. Yet you find the children splashing and splashing by the shores overlooking thatched mud houses and buildings that are only few and far between. It is not a pretty sight not even a delight in sight, especially at night. When the village sleeps and the battle with your mind begins.

I cry for my Delta because it could be so much more but here, we are like a cursed nation waiting to reach the promised land. Leaders blind to their plight, fattened pockets and swollen bellies, trading their souls, betraying their very own. To stop crying I must give just like my father, maybe I can affect on a faction, but I shall see smiles before I leave.

QUESTIONS THAT MATTER

I agree that we live to learn, that each passing day remarkably becomes a moment of reckoning. Different from days past, different from the days to come. Revelations come to pass, speculations surround, circumstances abound. The answers we find are the treasures for the day.
Each day I live, I try to give as much as I would try to receive yet emotions and people elude me. I want no distractions and you are quick to ask what distractions? No distractions from the questions that matter and the answers that validates it. The answers that remove the scales from my eyes, so I can see the gaps
I want to learn to bask in today's pleasures, knowing fully well that the music I dance to can change in tempo. That my dance steps much change accordingly rhythm against the beats subtle or fast, it is the dance of life. The dance that you cannot ignore because when the music stops. It stops for good

MY CHOICE

I choose to be happy; I choose to be content; I choose to be so much more. In the midst of stormy waters. The cold brushes my face in the

pouring rain. Making it hard to tell which are
tears or which is rain. Tears of pain are short
lived by determination to excel.
There are poor choices in the ones that we
voluntarily make. It is those ones that hurt the
most and sometimes leave you with regrets. Is it
not a good thing that regrets are short lived by
my determination to excel?
Life is unpredictable, life as we know is
mysterious. Armed with this knowledge and
blessed with experience, I take my stride, with
pride head up high, high in the clouds. Reeling
with laughter, laughter caused by my
determination to excel.

KARMA

To think that everything we do in life has an
effect on our lives can be scary, but looking at
the bright side, we can mould the future. What
this means is that when you play your role in life,
the reasonable way, the good way, it will pay off
ultimately.
I used to think that as I progress through life that
the clouds would give way to the perfect
rainbow, until I realized that we always want
something more. The choices we make, the
mistakes we learn from, and the experiences we
gain, open ours eyes further.
The journey never ends, it bends but it will never
stop. Just like a clock that ticks away with each

passing day. From dusk till dawn. The cycle continues, like a train on the tracks. We lose track of time. Until we have stopped and only then we can say that it is truly over.

HOPE PARK

When you re stressed and feeling less blessed, you cannot speak because you are numb and dumb from the pain. You cannot explain from all the strain. You wish it all goes down the drain with the pouring rain. You exclaim, so that one day you can claim that you had no clue, but you had to aim.
That it would all be better tough you sound bitter, on the other side you see glitter, and compare to your litter. That is when you write a long letter. The effect will determine the latter but in the now, all you want is a platter so that when you have had your fill, you can be bold enough to scatter to others who it seems stood to chatter.
In all of the sadness in a world of darkness there is always room for things to change. There you will find that gloom and doom is giving way for bloom. There you realize that no matter the size or slice of fate that is your share. There is a glimmer of hope, through the shimmer of light in the dark of night.
Where faith collides with fate to release the gift of a miracle and without an oracle, you see the end from the bend and you say it looks like I am

on the mend, now I can blend in with the crowd
and scream out loud that no matter how bad it
looked. I took a second look and said to myself.
It is not so bad Afterall.

HOT MESS

Sometimes we all find ourselves in a mess, not
just you but everything around you is a mess.
Whether it is the state of Bo' Jo's hair, the mess
of Brexit, the mess of killings on trumps side of
the plate or the state of my children's room after
a frenzied sugar rush
 Crush that it's messier on my side, as I decide
the best way to manage my relationships in a ship
that is constantly swerving against tempestuous
waves.
 I wave across to no one in particular as if help is
on the other side, then I realize what I really need
is a brush. A brush for my messy hair, I need to
brush away the fears and tears that follow each
breaking news from home and abroad.
Brush aside the things I cannot control yet find a
way to live with it. Brush away negativity in all
shades, shapes and shadows. Brush, Brush, Brush
till all the mess is gone and I can breathe again

DEATH IS DEATH.

We talk about death as if it's some plague that
affects others and not us.

We talk about death as if it is different
when someone popular or a pauper dies.
When you realize that death is imminent from the
day you are born, then you are blessed with a gift
that cannot shift.
When you accept that with death there is no
exception from conception to the actualization of
our lives purpose. Then and then only can your
realization become an elevation.
Death is death, young or old, it's cold and it will
mould you to humility like gravity that holds you
down without warning.
As death is bold and cold
I urge everyone to be bold.
To look death in the eye and say choose your
time and date without hate.
I will accept my fate and hope that I would be
remembered one way or another.

THE GREAT ONES

Are they born? Or are they made? Or like the
great debate of philosophers, psychologists, and
scientists. Is it nature or nurture? The questions
arise and the answers vary from the north, south,
east, or west. Black or white, they stand tall
above their kind. Ambitious, conscientious,
exalted, and often wealthy. Their praises are sung
on the lips of many.
Many suffer a great fall, sometimes there is a
comeback, some die in their prime, some live

long enough then bow to death honourably. The world is a stage, they choose their role and play for all till the last page. They leave indelible marks in the sands of time.

The beautiful ones may not yet be born, but the great ones come and go. For never shall the world lack the luminous and glorious appeal of the great ones.

SOLITUDE

When I am alone, I see that which I didn't see before. I capture moments, I see clearer, I make believe, I do what I want to do. The beauty of silence is that it is away from the maddening crowd. The freedom to be myself, to think, to reflect, re-appraise and figure things out. This to me is priceless and therefore golden.

ROAMING

The state of the mind at any given time can never be blank. It ticks like a clock it, breezes through thoughts, wishes, dreams, regrets, anxieties, anticipations, fear, joy, and pain.

I find solace somewhere between these realms because somehow, It is a wonderful feeling to conceive, plan and put into action.

It is all in your head. That is where it starts. It might be a glimpse or a snippet. The seed is sown and that is where it all begins. The mind is the ultimate conception.

THIS LITTLE LIGHT OF MINE.

If I shine, why do you whine?
We all have our parts to play and paths to take.
God being so kind, bestowed on us all.
We are fragments of one, helpless without the
other, unified for perfection.
For that purpose, are here.
Join the chain, forget the pain, let it be your gain
to be a part of the mortal discovery.

THE SEARCH

In my quest for a niche, I find myself in different
evolving facets of life, all with their own little
lessons. To really understand, to be a teacher, one
must truly experience enough to take you through
the tears, fears, and laughter.
There is a clearer picture to where we are headed.
We are not responsible for our being here ''The
greater one is''. Until we know this our souls are
lost in a frolic of their own.

WE, ONCE, WERE BABIES.

The first cry that tears into the silence of the
hospital walls, marks the arrival of yet another
one of us. I would love to know what if feels like
to join the world because I cannot remember.

Can it really be described? Almost immediately the mother is engulfed in a euphoria of joy. It transcends any form of human experience. It is spiritual, an unseen force that stays from womb to tomb.
It is an unending bond from the cradle to the first signs of independence. The mind is built, the heart is moulded against the backdrop of the everything and everyone around.
It brings to mind the big question why are we here? To procreate, to provide, build foundations upon which destinies are created. That circular chain is formed.
For this reason, I say I was once a baby, I will make babies that will in turn make babies. The story never really ends does it?

EXPECTATIONS

It is not different from the ordinary plans of setting out to do what you truly desire. Having a conscious awareness of the pros and cons that will eventually set a pendulum of events with the ultimate pay off success.
Success, being an elevated state of triumph and victory. The journey takes centre stage and is heightened by prospects that must remain in view. Strength to strength, glory to glory
To succeed and stay a success is the true test of achievement. This is often characterized by the zest and zeal to remain on top.

BY THE WAYSIDE

Dreams are but a mirage until they become a reality. Most plans fall by the wayside because they lack the fundamental foresight, a foundation upon which these dreams can thrive. They are blurred by fear of imminent difficulties and risks, that so many are unwilling to take.
On the other hand while some toil day and night waiting for an opportunity to grab or a gap to fill, Some stare, talk and make ridicule of aspirations and unborn dreams. What exactly is a better position to be in?
The answer is to embark on a journey bearing in mind that someday the tide will bring you to a fruitful shore. Life is a roller coaster of events, Time waits for no man, the time to act is now.

THE BEAUTY OF LIFE

The beauty of life is that being who you are is naturally uncontrollable, but on realizing who you are, you then decide where that takes you. This decision requires being in touch with your inner self as against the forces of nature. Then comes the highs and lows, which probably is the greatest battle of all times. It is what we live with, experience or sometimes part with. It is also the different issues people come to terms with that we may never experience ourselves. Simply put, Life is all about the puzzles we solve

and the puzzles that spring up just after one is
solved. What we should do, is to hold on to
pleasant memories, which are often short lived
anyway.
Life is pretty much like going down a slide, the
rush and the decline and the never-ending cycle
of events. There is a time and place for
everything so we must cry the tears that come
with joy and the tears that come with pain, enjoy
the laughter that comes with true happiness but
most importantly seize the moment because it
might be the most remarkable, helping you
eliminate that option of regret. That soft whisper
'If only I had known.

BIRDSONG

I went out looking for birds. But every inch I
took drove them further away.
I keep trying to capture them but I couldn't have
my way.
Then I said to myself, Wait a minute I can hear
them sing.
In an instant I am transfixed in a melody,
followed by their harmony.
I capture this song instead and together with the
tranquil rhythmic flow of the cray waters.
I am reminded of the fact that sometimes in life.
We search for something to no avail only to find
something more beautiful.
And There is nothing more beautiful than a bird

song on a beautiful day.

DANCING WITH THE BREEZE

It was a slit through the curtains that shifted my gaze. As if in a daze my eyes are fixed on this dance.
She twirled and waved, giving way to intensity as the branches and leaves chose to tango.
The breeze swirled, I moved closer from my freeze, but wait a minute she has always danced.
It's the first time I notice.

As if to impress, with an express twist she pauses and gives a final bow.
I
It was a lovely distraction,
I am grateful for interaction
It is worthy of an ovation.

THE HOPE THAT SPRING BROUGHT

As the land was ravaged and rampaged with the unknown, fears gave way to tears. The rainbow became a symbol of hope, a light at the end of the tunnel.
As the world was swept by winds of change and we all wept under the pressure. It is a pleasure to see the flowers blossom.
As life takes a new meaning, it is the dawn of an

era that eradicates mind sets that have raced against time, misplaced priorities, broken homes, broken dreams, missing links in broken systems. As but at last, a bridge to the other side. The world holds it breath, pushes the restart button and the cleansing begins.
As I take a walk to be healed by the scenery amidst all the greenery. All I can think to say is that the worst may not be over, but this is the hope that spring brought.

THE CROSSROADS

Through my restless and sleepless night. I found myself on the verge. At the very point where I am about to jump. To jump into the journey. To rescue what seems to be drowning in a current of emotions that seems all so familiar. There is a reason why you master certain things maybe it's because you have come down the same road several times before and you reach the cross roads where you have to decide again if your journey is a retreat or one of surrender. I stand in my truth with a clear vision that it's almost blinding.

I am at loss for words as I feel myself recoiling into my shell. A dark lonely place but a secure one, nonetheless. If love is real and hope is alive then my faith will lead me to my fate. My tears mingle with every fear. I take a step guided by a contrite heart. All these years gone by, all that I have given will not return to me void as I seek answers. knowing that in the end I will celebrate love in all its glory and entirety.

Index of First Lines

L

Let me carry my cross, 21

S

Sometimes we all find ourselves in a mess, 28

T

The beauty of life is that being who you are is, 35
The first cry that tears into the silence, 32
The lost ones, 11
Through my restless and sleepless night, 38
To think that everything we do in life, 25

V

Victim of beauty, 11

W

We talk about death, 29
What do you do with your time?, 16
What is the value of a woman with beauty?, 19
When I am alone, 31
When you re stressed and feeling less, 26

Printed in Great Britain
by Amazon

85711780R00027